Mount St. Helens
A Mountain Explodes

Gary Miller

Rigby®

A Harcourt Achieve Imprint

www.Rigby.com
1-800-531-5015

March 20, 1980

The Mount St. Helens **volcano** has been quiet for more than 100 years. It hasn't **erupted** since 1857. Since then the mountain has slept peacefully, with its top wrapped in snow.

This year the mountain began to change. Small **earthquakes** shook the mountain. It may be ready to wake from its long sleep.

Today at 3:45 P.M., an earthquake caused a snow **avalanche** on the volcano. The strength of the earthquake could mean trouble. It may mean that the volcano will erupt. Who knows what will happen! Any changes will be written in this volcano log.

In early 1980, Mount St. Helens' snowy peak rises above forests near Spirit Lake, Washington.

March 27, 1980

Since March 20, many earthquakes have shaken Mount St. Helens. Scientists are recording 20 quakes every hour. Now they are sure the volcano will erupt.

This morning at 11:20 A.M., an airplane flew over the volcano. The captain saw a hole in the ice cap near the top. At 12:30 P.M., people near the volcano heard a loud **explosion**. Smoke and **ash** began to rise from the mountain. By 2:00 P.M., the cloud rose 7,000 feet, which is much higher in the air than the tallest building in the world.

Scientists recorded the number of quakes each hour with tools like this one

By the afternoon of March 27, 1980, the cloud had risen 7,000 feet in the air.

Hundreds of people live and work near the volcano. Other people are vacationing there. Scientists are worried that Mount St. Helens is a real danger. Today police and firefighters told people to leave the area. The roads near the volcano are closed to cars.

Roadblocks stopped travelers from getting close to the mountain.

Scientists closely watched the volcano using special tools.

People might not know this, but the biggest risk if the volcano erupts is flooding. Hot **lava** that flows from the volcano could melt the ice cap on the mountain. If this happens, water will rush down the mountain. Streams and rivers will rise. Luckily, people are safe for now.

May 15, 1980

For the past month, hundreds of earthquakes and small explosions have shaken Mount St. Helens. The north side of the volcano now has a large, cracking bump on it. This bump, called a bulge, is 300 feet high. Hot, melting rock and gases are moving underneath the bulge. Scientists fear that the bulge might cause a **landslide** or that it could explode.

May 18, 1980

Today it happened. At 8:32 A.M., an earthquake caused a huge landslide. Much of the northwest side of the mountain fell. Then the mountain exploded. A cloud of ash rose over 62,000 feet high in the air. That's much higher in the air than even an airplane flies. The area all around the mountain has been destroyed.

A cloud of ash rose more than 62,000 feet in the air on May 18, 1980.

May 19, 1980

The volcano's blast created winds of 300 miles per hour. The heat of the winds reached 660 degrees Fahrenheit. The blast knocked down or buried almost 230 square miles of trees.

For many miles around the mountain, the forest is gone. Only a few dead trees can be seen above the rocks and ash.

The blast knocked down thousands of trees.

Before Mount
St. Helens
erupted

After Mount
St. Helens
erupted

May 20, 1980

Huge walls of mud called **lahars** swept down the valleys all day. The lahars pulled trees out by their roots, buried the land under tons of mud, and destroyed nearly 200 homes and 27 bridges.

Everything is covered in 2-5 inches of ash. There is so much ash in the air that it's already covering parts of Colorado. That's 3 states away!

Lahars damaged homes in the mountain valleys.

Bulge

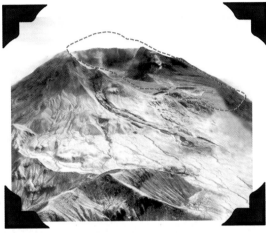

Mount St. Helens was shorter by 1,314 feet after the blast, which removed the *bulge*.

The eruption has changed the shape of the mountain. It is 1,314 feet shorter now. The flow of new lava is changing the mountain, too. Hour by hour, it is beginning to build up again.

May 18, 2005

It's been 25 years since the big eruption in 1980, and signs of everyday life on Mount St. Helens have returned. Some animals quickly returned to the area, while other animals took longer. Seeds that the wind carried from nearby places landed here. Those seeds grew in the rich soil. Flowers and other plants have sprung up.

Life returns to the mountain

Steam still rises from the Mount St. Helens volcano today.

Today Mount St. Helens is still a bubbling volcano, and small eruptions and earthquakes keep happening. Luckily, there haven't been any large eruptions since 1980. The mountain seems quiet, but it might explode again.

We'll keep watching Mount St. Helens and recording its changes in volcano logs. We'll be ready when and if this sleeping giant decides to wake up and roar once more.

GLOSSARY

ash kind of dust thrown out of a volcano when the volcano erupts

avalanche large mass of snow and ice that slides down a mountain

earthquake sudden shaking, moving, and cracking of the earth

erupt throw out lava, ash, and gases suddenly

explosion sudden blast that makes a loud noise and can hurt things

lahars huge walls of mud

landslide rock and soil that slide down the side of a mountain

lava melted rock that flows out of a volcano

volcano a hole in the earth that steam, ash, and lava come through